Also available from Jon Zens...

The Pastor Has No Clothes!
Moving From Clergy-Centered Church to Christ-Centered Ekklesia
(Spring 2011)

What's With Paul And Women?
Unlocking the Cultural Background to 1 Timothy 2
(2010)

A Church Building Every 1/2 Mile
What Makes American Christianity Tick?
(2008)

PRE-EKKLESIA PUBLISHED

"This Is My Beloved Son, Hear Him":
The Foundation for New Covenant Ethics & Ecclesiology
Searching Together, 1997

Moses & the Millennium:
An Appraisal of Christian Reconstructionism
Searching Together, 1988

Desiring Unity...Finding Division:
Lessons from the 19th Century Restorationist Movement
Searching Together, 1986

The above are available at www.jonzens.com

What Others Are Saying . . .

This critique of *LoveWins* by Jon Zens represents a penetrating analysis that masterfully raises a series of pertinent points, each derived from the scriptures themselves. These points not only individually challenge Bell's process of suggesting that salvation will in the end include everybody, but collectively constitute a sound refutation of the conclusions found in *LoveWins*.

—Dennis J. Mulkey, author of the
forthcoming *Treason Against Christ: A
Summons to Reclaim the Authentic Identity of
the Word of God* (Tate, 2011)

In *Christ Minimized?* author Jon Zens clearly and biblically refutes the major thesis of Rob Bell's best-selling book, *Love Wins*. Jon shows us that it is far more biblical to emphasize the depth of God's love for sinners who trust in Christ than it is to focus on the breadth of God's love for sinners who never come to Christ. In short, Jon Zens rebuts *Love Wins* to show that *Christ wins*.

—Wade Burleson, pastor, Emmanuel Baptist
Church, Enid OK

There is an inherent danger in heresy hunting. Sooner or later, the hunter invariably turns into the hunted. The raging, incoherent spirit and zealotry of many within the

Christian religious establishment in response to *Love Wins*, alarms me more than the merits, or lack thereof, in Rob Bell's work. In the midst of the spastic fulminations from within "evangelical orthodoxy" (a highly debatable concept), it is refreshing to find a dispassionate response to *Love Wins* such as what Jon Zens has provided. In a concise, reachable, readable, and disciplined biblical perspective way, Jon addresses the theology of *Love Wins* and finds it ultimately unreconcilable with the full counsel of scripture.

—**Dr. Stephen Crosby**, author of *The Silent Killers of Faith: Overcoming Legalism & Performance-Based Religion and Praise, Worship & the Presence of God: A New Covenant Perspective*, North Carolina

I am pleased to commend Jon's critique of *Love Wins* as a fair, and much needed exposure of the deeply flawed theology in this book, with it's re-packaging of the old error of universalism, or the salvation of everyone. The approach of *Love Wins* is subtle, with selected scriptures quoted and plausibly presented so as to deceive undiscerning readers. Truth is the first casualty as the clear waters of the Gospel are muddied by it's speculative and ambiguous approach. One has to wonder if "another gospel" is being presented via a mystical approach to salvation, implying that even those who resist or reject the Gospel may yet be saved. The book also has some serious omissions in relation to vital biblical subjects, such as the eternal consequences of sin, God's holiness, the blood of Christ, and His substitutionary death and atonement. Jon exposes the questionable use of scripture in *Love Wins* with grace, and relevant scripture passages are positively interpreted in their rightful contexts, thus pointing readers toward the whole counsel of Christ.

— **Graham Wood**, Retired Government Worker, UK

When I read the title of Jon's response to Rob Bell's book *Love Wins*, I immediately was captured by Jon's longing to see Jesus Christ made supreme and central to the *ekkelsia* of God, His body. Christ should be Lord and Leader among His people, in fact, He should be the very Life of His people. Jesus Christ is not a set of teachings that are apart from Himself, but He is the real food, the real water, and the real life. Christ desires to live supremely and centrally in His body!

In *Christ Minimized?* Jon astutely brings out the centrality of Christ as he reflects on the message of Rob Bell's controversial book. Jon looks at what Bell writes and searches the Christ of scripture to give a more balanced view that neither those who subscribe to "eternal torment" nor "universalism" usually consider. Jon's approach is to see what Scripture really says and lay it before the body and let the *ekklesia* see the reality of what was written to the first century church. Jon comes with a heart, like all believers past and present, that all would know our Lord, but realizing that while God so loved the world that He sent His Son, not everyone would believe in Him. What is the fate of those who do not trust in Jesus Christ? Can we accept "eternal torment" as perpetrated by the institutional church, or does scripture say something different, such as "perish"? I am more inclined to go with what the Scriptures seem to say.

As Jon points out, opinions can often be masked by the dangers of reading our current modern and traditional practices into the interpretation of the Bible. Jon has been uniquely gifted of the Lord to help the body search the scripture and allow His Spirit to interpret it for us. We can often focus on a partial Scripture and limit or silence the witness of other Scriptures. Perhaps the reason we are called to search Scripture together is so that Christ in us can give us better insight as to what He really wants us to know. It is only by the Spirit of God that we receive a balanced teaching in the body and the fuller expression of the life of Christ in His people.

The message of *Love Wins* is yet one additional voice in the powder keg of emotion in the religious debates of history regarding eternal torment or universalism, debates that sadly have divided the body and left a trail of tears. Jon brings to the table the voice of balance, the voice of insight, and the voice of reality that can only be Christ in him.

Christ is bigger than any of us can imagine. In the end Jon humbly confesses that "no position is airtight, and there are always a few Scriptures that seem to challenge every view." In my own study, learning and yearning to hear Christ, the words Jon shares echo my own as well. In fact, it is surprising how what I read are the same conclusions I have also come to acknowledge. Only the Spirit can do that. May Father give us spiritual sight to see more of His Son in His body.

—**John Scott Wilson**, blogger at http://
johnswilson3.wordpress.com, Texas

Christ Minimized? — The title of Jon's response to *Love Wins* by Rob Bell—says it all. With the plethora of debate surrounding Bell's book, it is refreshing to see the conversation directed back to the crucial element in this debate. The minimization of Jesus Christ is the central issue at hand! Jon masterfully directs us back to the seriousness and reality of the wrath of God that is, and will be in the future, revealed against those who suppress the truth of God. Jesus Christ is indeed the very incarnation of God's truth!

While Jon skillfully brings the conversation back to the importance of what we do with Jesus Christ here in this life, he also challenges some of the more traditional views of hell and the afterlife that Bell is reacting to in his book. Jon's work is a much-needed addition to this all-important discussion, and I guarantee that your thinking will be challenged through this conversation. Mine certainly was.

— **Jamal Jivanjee**, www.jamaljivanjee.com,
Tennessee

Jon Zens can be contacted at:
jzens@searchingtogether.org or 715-338-2796

Christ Minimized?

Christ Minimized?

A Response to
Rob Bell's *Love Wins*

^{By} Jon Zens

Forward By Edward Fudge

Ekklesia Press, 2011

Christ Minimized
by Jon Zens

Library of Congress Control Number: 2011944140

Publisher's Cataloging-in-Publication data

Zens, Jon H.
    Christ minimized? : a response to Rob Bell's love wins / by Jon Zens ; foreword by Edward Fudge.
    p. cm.
    ISBN 978-0-9827446-7-3

1. Judgment of God. 2. Hell --Christianity. 3. Hell --Biblical teaching..
4. Future life --Christianity. 5. Future life --Biblical teaching. I. Fudge, Edward. II. Title.

BT836.3 Z46 2011
236/.25 --dc22
2011944140

This volume is printed on acid free paper and meets ANSI Z39.48 standards.

Cover design and layout by: Kathy Huff & Rafael Polendo
Printed in the United States of America

Omaha, NE

CONTENTS:

DEDICATION

I would like to dedicate *Christ Minimized?* to Benjamin
& Kathy Brooks, whose kindness and hospitality have
refreshed us on numerous occasions! "God is not unjust
to forget your work and the love which you showed to his
name, having served the saints, and
you continue to serve." Hebrews 6:10

FOREWORD

Every author could wish for the notoriety generated by Rob Bell's book *Love Wins*! And most of us can honestly confess at least a trace of envy because of the unfulfilled wish. Myriads of writers have written reviews, responses, analyses and replies to Bell. Some of them betray unworthy motives that discredit their own work and raise suspicion regarding their integrity. Some who attack Bell the most ferociously admit that they have not even read his book.

However, it is pleasant to report that others who critique Bell's book spend many hours trying to understand accurately what Bell actually says, and then to critique that with intelligence (basing their remarks and their responses on facts) and with grace (disagreeing, when necessary, with Bell's position rather than merely bashing the man). Regardless of their position—in terms either of the doctrine being discussed, or with respect to their position of honor within their own faith community and the larger church in general—those are the men and women who earn our respect and who merit our trust. Jon Zens exemplifies that second type of person.

Jon does not attempt to be exhaustive in his analysis. He writes in response to requests from brothers and sisters in his own sphere of influence, for people who want a brief but careful synopsis of Bell's position, and a word they can seriously reflect upon regarding the trustworthiness of Bell's position. Jon meets those criteria splendidly, even remarking about a few subjects that obviously are of greater concern in his own circle than they are to many in the church-at-large. (That is a statement of my own opinion, and it says nothing about the importance of those particular issues.)

I met Jon in Nashville, Tennessee, in 1979. Through three decades, Jon has shown himself willing to re-examine old views and, when necessary based on evidence, to exchange them for new ones. I appreciate that in him, and it predisposes me to want to trust his judgment in matters about which I know little at the time. Let us hope that brother Bell will be equally open to reconsider what he says in *Love Wins* — always to the glory of God.

—Edward William Fudge, author of
The Fire that Consumes, Houston, TX

CHRIST MINIMIZED?

A Response to Rob Bell's Love Wins: A Book About Heaven, Hell, and the Fate of Every Person Who Ever Lived

This book brought about furor and buzz even before it was released! As a leading evangelical with quite a following, for him to tender the idea that all people might be ultimately made right with God was highly controversial. Among believers, we ought to be able to discuss a range of issues, but, as Bell observes, "Some communities don't permit open, honest inquiry about the things that matter most" (p. ix). Bell has written several previous books, and I really profited from his *Sex God: Exploring the Endless Connections Between Sexuality and Spirituality* (2007).

Normally, I would hesitate to react to a book like this, but a number of people have requested my response to it. Given the main subject matter of *Love Wins*, it actually affords the opportunity to touch on a number of matters that may help the brothers and sisters in Christ clarify and re-think some traditional understandings of scripture.

I had to chuckle loudly when Bell was going over the ideas connected to heaven being *somewhere else*, and he came to this one: "I've heard pastors answer, 'It will be unlike anything we can comprehend, like a church service that goes on forever,' causing some to think, 'That sounds more like hell'" (p. 25).

Was John a "Pastor"?

This may seem like a strange place to start, but I think it sets the tone for the rest of my analysis. It seems that Bell wants to link the apostle John to our traditional profession of "the pastorate." Thus he suggests that the *Book of Revelation* came "from a pastor named John" (p.111; cf. pp. 48,135). When discussing the purpose of *Revelation* he feels that it was "written by a real pastor" to the "people in this church that John pastored" (p. 112).

In the course of his discussion of hell, Bell mentions that "the pastor's job, among other things, is to help family and friends properly honor the dead" (p. 71). Bell connected his job as a pastor[1] to John four times in his book *Love Wins*. Now I don't think it is a stretch to believe that many readers of this book will naturally picture the apostle John fitting into this job description, presiding at funerals where the dead are honored. However, the traditional "job of pastor" was unknown in the early church. Further, there is no New Testament (from here on NT) evidence that John was "a pastor." As I noted in my book, *The Pastor Has No Clothes*, in response to Eugene Peterson's claim that John pastored the seven churches in *Revelation* 2-3, and that the seven letters were "sermons" John delivered to them:

[1] In September, 2011, Rob Bell announced that he was resigning from Mars Hill Bible Church in Grandville, Michigan (http://global.christianpost.com/news/love-wins-author-rob-bell-tells-mars-hill-his-departure-is-no-surprise-56454/ and www.wzzm13.com/news/article/179938/14/rob-bell-leaving-mars-hill-church-in-december). Apparently in December, 2011, he is moving his family to the Los Angeles area to work in the writing and production of a TV series (http://eugenecho.com/2011/09/29/rob-bell-is-going-hollywood-and-i-give-him-two-thumbs-up/).

There is no explicit evidence that John was "the pastor" of the seven congregations mentioned in *Revelation* 2 & 3. It is yet another case where Peterson, like so many others, "reads" modern practice *into* the NT text by suggesting Christ's words to these seven churches were "sermons" by John.... "The pastor" as defined by Eugene in his book simply is not to be found in the NT documents. Yet visible Christianity has become anchored to the concept and physical presence of clergy or "the pastor" (pp. 86-87).

I would suggest that throughout *Love Wins* certain ideas are connected with selected scriptures, but there is little to no reason to believe that there is any viable connection between the two.

Strange Sentiments

In the course of this book some very curious interpretations of the Bible are expressed. I have difficulty squaring such ideas with the revelation of Christ in scripture. Here are seven examples:

◊ When Mama Zebedee came to Jesus to request prominent seats for her sons in the future, *Love Wins* posits that "she understood heaven to be about partnering with God to make a new and better world, one with increasingly complex and expansive expressions and dimensions of *shalom*, creativity, beauty, and design" (p. 47).

   The context indicates that she was focused on future glory for her sons. To put the author's expanded conjectures into her understanding is a real stretch, to say the least. The author's words do not seem sensitive to anything actually rooted in this Gospel story.

◊ "Jesus makes no promise," *Love Wins* says, "that in the blink of an eye we will suddenly become totally different people" (p. 50). It rejects "the idea that in the blink of an eye we will automatically become totally different people who 'know' everything" (p. 51).

What Paul said in Philippians 3:20-21, however, challenges this opinion. "And we eagerly await a Savior from heaven, the Lord Jesus Christ, who, by the power that enables him to bring everything under his control, will transform our lowly bodies so that they will be like his glorious body." 1 Corinthians 15:51-52 sure sounds like the blink of an eye! "We shall not all sleep, but we shall all be changed—in a flash, in the twinkling of an eye, at the last trumpet. For the trumpet will sound, the dead in Christ will be raised imperishable, and we shall be changed." The transition from this age to the age to come will occur when Jesus returns in glory, and we will see him as he is (1 John 3:2). We know in part now, but when he comes back it will be face-to-face in the age to come (1 Cor. 13:12). When he returns the saints will be glorified (2 Thes. 1:10; cf. Rom. 8:30). Their mortal bodies will become immortal via resurrection.

Jesus certainly implied a radical change in our existence by saying that he would raise up all of his people on the last day, thus ushering in the age to come—a New Heaven/New Earth where there is no curse (John 6:39; Rev. 22:3).

◊ *Love Wins* makes the striking statement that a world without sin "could take some getting used to" (p. 51).

Such a statement would do well to consider Paul's perspective that when the saints are "glorified," the presence of sin in their resurrected bodies will be eradicated. The New Heaven/New Earth where Christ is the Light and Life is not a setting where the inhabitants have to "get used to" anything. Rather, the Bride will be visibly married to the Groom forever in their glorious habitat together. Heaven and earth will come together as one, with the Lamb at the center.

◊ *Love Wins* makes some remarks that blur a clear distinction made in the NT. "God is doing a new work through Jesus, calling all people to human solidarity. Everybody is a brother, a sister. Equals, children of the God who shows no favoritism" (pp. 75-76).

By his cross and resurrection Jesus removed the law so that a "new humanity"—a "new creation"— a counter-culture would be expressed in the midst of a fallen creation. This "new humanity" is defined as the children of Abraham—as those who have faith in Christ (Gal. 3:28). It is only "in Christ" that there is no Jew or Gentile, bond or free, male or female. The redemptive sociological healing that accomplishes "human solidarity" is found only in the *ekklesia*. Only in the body of Christ will you find brothers and sisters who are equals. The "children of God" are only those who believe in Jesus, not "everybody" on earth.

◊ Along these same lines, Bell makes the sweeping remark that baptism and the Lord's Supper are actually for everybody. "These rituals are true for us, because they're true for everybody. They unite us, because they unite everybody.... These are signs, glimpses, and tastes of what is true for all peop[in all places at all times" (p. 157).

These are the author's thoughts and are rooted nowhere in Christ's revelation. Baptism and the Lord's Supper are for the *ekklesia*—those who are entering into and basking in the life of Christ. These two activities only have significance *where faith in Christ is active*. To say that they are equally applicable to everybody is to render faith in, and love for, Christ irrelevant.

◊ "Some people have so much baggage with regard to the name 'Jesus' that when they encounter the mystery present in all of creation—grace, peace, love, acceptance, healing, forgiveness— the last thing they are inclined to name it is 'Jesus'" (p. 159).

Such language as "the mystery present in all of creation" seems to be a nebulous, vacuous generalization. I have no problem with Jesus revealing himself to folks without a Bible and without a missionary, but it is an unveiling of the person of Christ, not some indefinable "mystery" in the creation. Jesus is the "mystery" of God. The "mystery" is a *person*—not "it's" like grace, peace and love.

◊ *Love Wins* suggests that there is still the possibility that Sodom and Gomorrah will be redeemed. Somehow it extracts "hope" for Sodom out of Jesus' words to Capernaum that on the *day of judgment* "it will be more tolerable for Sodom and Gomorrah than for you" (Matt. 10:15).

The *day of judgment* is turned into a day of redemption! "There's still hope.... And if there's still hope for Sodom and Gomorrah, what does that say about all the other Sodoms and Gomorrahs?" (pp.84-85). The NT, on the other hand, teaches that what happened long ago in the destruction of Sodom and Gomorrah was an example of the judgment still to come on the ungodly. "He condemned the cities of Sodom and Gomorrah to destruction by reducing them to ashes, having made them an example to those who would live ungodly thereafter" (2 Pet. 2:6, *NASB*). "Just as Sodom and Gomorrah and the cities around them, since they in the same way as these [false teachers] indulged in gross immorality and went after strange flesh, are exhibited as an example, in undergoing the punishment of eternal fire" (Jude 7, *NASB*).

Can Christ the King Overcome A Flat Tire?

Love Wins asks these questions, "If our salvation, our future, our destiny is dependent on others bringing the message to us, teaching us, showing us—what happens if they don't do their part? What if the missionary gets a flat tire? This raises another, far more disturbing question: Is your future in someone else's hands?" (p. 9).

Would the eternal purpose of God in Christ to secure and maintain a Bride for the Son—a purpose in which the Lord works everything out according to the counsel of his will—be left in the hands of frail human beings and adverse circumstances (Eph. 1:11; 3:11)? Absolutely not! If Father intends to reveal Christ to a person, he will oversee all of the circumstances. If someone fails to speak when they should, or if a car breaks down in the middle of the road—the Lord will find other means to accomplish his plans.

Remember Paul's encounter with Christ? Here was a man who was opposed to Jesus and had authority to harass and hurt believers. He was on a path to continue his persecution when out of the blue he was knocked to the ground by radiant light from the Lord. No gospel tracts. No *Four Spiritual Laws*. No preacher. No missionary. No flat tires. Jesus found the vessel he had chosen, and thus in Paul this scripture was fulfilled, "I made myself known to people who were not looking for me; I was found by those who were not asking me for help" (Isa. 65:1).

God's purpose to save a numberless multitude in Christ is not left in anyone's hands —except the Lord's. As Jonah exclaimed, "Salvation is of the Lord." Jesus said, "No person is able to come to me unless the Father who sent me draws him, and I will raise him up in the last day.... Therefore I have already said to you, 'No person is able to come to me unless it has been given to him of the Father' " (John 6:44, 65). Jesus will not lose one of his people —they will all be raised up to life in the last day (John 6:39).

Straw Persons

In two key areas, *Love Wins* seems to create straw persons in order to make its position more appealing. First, it contrasts its view that includes everybody with traditional notions. The other view is characterized as one in which only a "select few," "only a few," a "select number" make it to the good place (pp. viii, 2, 3, 103, 110).

This is an inaccurate picture. The NT presents an ultimate scenario where there is a "great multitude which no one can count, from every tribe, kindred and tongue" standing before the Lamb (Rev. 7:9, 19:6-7). The promise to Abraham will be fulfilled—his seed "in Christ" will be numberless, like the sand on the beach and the stars in the sky. The final host of those purchased by the blood of the Lamb is anything but "only a few"!

Secondly, *Love Wins* portrays those who pronounce judgment on "sinners" in terms of "people who don't believe what they believe" (p. 95). He boils it all down to making it look like those who are condemned are "people who don't believe the right things" (p.82). In a *Time* magazine article, author Jon Meacham notes that Bell "is unclear on whether the redemption promised in Christian tradition is limited to those who meet the tests of the church" ("Is Hell Dead?," April 25, 2011, p.40).

Such depictions are very distant from the real issue. Of course, there are groups who have a list you must conform to, or in their eyes you will perish. But it must be underscored that the vital issue is this: *people will be judged, not because they did not believe the right things or fell short of the church's criteria, but because they did not believe and trust in Jesus Christ.* Jesus taught that the work of the Spirit in the Gospel age was to convince people of "sin, because they do not believe in me" (John 16:9). *It's all about the person of Jesus, not about the right things, doctrines, and superficial lists created by religious groups*!

Partially Cites Scripture

Throughout the book, *Love Wins* will mention a scripture, but omits information in it that contradicts or challenges its viewpoint. Matthew 13:30 is cited and it is said, "Jesus speaks of a harvest at the 'end of the age' " (p. 30). But these words of Jesus are omitted: "I will say to the reapers, 'First gather up the tares and bind them in bundles to burn them up.' " That sounds like some folks *are* going to be destroyed! Things that are burned up do not have another chance for salvation, do they?

Love Wins points to the *Book of Revelation*, and notes, "It ends with two chapters describing a new city, a new creation, a new world that God makes, right here in the midst of this one" (p.112). This is seen as the final "buoyant, hopeful vision" in the Bible. Yet Revelation 21:8 is left out—"but for the cowardly and unbelieving and abominable and murderers and immoral persons and sorcerers and idolaters and all liars, their part will be in the lake that burns with fire and brimstone, which is the second death." This part of the story is seemingly swept under the rug, as if it does not exist!

Leaves the Wrong Impression

There are a number of occasions where *Love Wins* alludes to scripture, but the reader is left with the wrong impression about the matter at hand.

1 Corinthians 3:9-15: *Love Wins* sees this passage as a general statement about the Lord's overview of "each person's" work (p. 49). But Paul spends the first four chapters of 1 Corinthians dealing with the problem of believers clustering around personalities. In chapter 3, Paul makes a clear distinction between the foundation (Jesus Christ), the *result* (the believing Corinthians), and the *means* (people like Apollos, Peter and Paul): "we are God's fellow workers; you are God's field, God's building" (1 Cor. 3:9). Thus, this section is not about all believers' works being examined, but specifically about the scrutiny of workers' labors who build upon the foundation of Christ (for an excellent discussion of 1 Cor. 3 see Robert L. Dabney, *Discussions: Evangelical and Theological* [1890], London, Banner of Truth Trust, 1967, Vol. 1, pp. 551ff.).

Amos 9: The author uses this text in a list of Old Testament (OT) verses to suggest the possibility of "restoration" in the age to come (p. 87). In other words, that people will have a chance for redemption after they die. But Amos 9 was cited in Acts 15:15-18 as referring to the inclusion of believing Gentiles now in this age.

1 Corinthians 15: *Love Wins* believes that when Paul said, "in Christ all will be made alive," he had "everybody" in mind (p. 134). But there is good reason to question this interpretation. *Love Wins* left out Paul's immediate qualifier that followed his above remark by saying, "but each in his own order: Christ the first fruits, after that those who are Christ's at his coming" (1 Cor. 15:23).

What Did "World" Mean In First Century Judaism?

A lot of confusion is created when people assume that the word "world" (Greek, *kosmos*) as used in the NT is *numerical*, thus meaning "every man, woman and child who has ever lived." This use sees "world" as *quantitative*, as referring to a huge number of people. But in many NT contexts, "world" is used in a *qualitative* manner in reference to that which is *non-Jewish*.

John 3:16, "God so loved the world...." Who was Jesus speaking to? Nicodemus was a bigoted Jewish leader who believed that Israel was the exclusive object of God's love. When he heard the word "world" connected to God's love, he would have wanted to cover his ears. To him, "world" meant "everything that is not Jewish," or "that which is outside of Judaism." It was a very negative category in which all Gentiles were regarded as "dogs," and certainly as "unclean" people not worthy of God's love.

John 4:42, "Savior of the world." In this context a Samaritan woman had been quite surprised when a Jewish man spoke to her and requested a drink of water. She knew that Samaritans were hated by the Jews. When Jesus revealed himself to her as the Messiah, she knew that this Redeemer was not just for Jews. She told her village about this Jesus, and they came to hear from him themselves. They were thrilled to learn that Messiah had brought salvation not only to Israel, but also to believing "non-Jews" as well. This is what they meant when they testified, "we have heard for ourselves, and we know that this man really is the Savior of the world."

Romans 11:15, "For if their [the Jews] rejection be the reconciliation of the world [Gentiles], what will their [the Jews] acceptance be but life from the dead?" This is yet another passage where the word "world" is used *qualitatively* rather than *quantitatively*. The sense is not "every person in the world," but all that is non-Jewish. In Romans 11:11-15 "world" and "Gentiles" are used interchangeably. Paul addressed here one of the major issues encountered by the early church. The OT had clearly foretold that the Messiah would be a light for all the nations. That God's love should extend beyond Palestine to embrace the whole "world" was a hard pill for Jews to swallow. This tension is a key to understanding most of the NT contexts where the word "world" is found.

Resurrection or Afterlife?

There is a crying need for more careful thought about the centrality of Christ's resurrection (which guaranteed ours too) in the NT. *Love Wins* affirms the importance in scripture of the resurrection (p. 61). However, some of his other remarks on the "afterlife" are shaped by theological traditions that need careful examination.

For example, regarding Luke 20, Bell notes, "when Jesus is asked about the afterlife, he refers in his response to 'those who are considered worthy of taking part in the age to come'" (p. 13). It must be underscored that when most readers of *Love Wins* see the word "after-life," their minds will go immediately to what happens when you die. But that is precisely not what Jesus is being asked about. The discussion is about the great day—the final day of history as we know it—the last day—of the resurrection of the just and the unjust (Acts 24:15).

I think it is safe to say that from roughly 1850 – 1990, the key question that emerged in connection with reaching the lost was, "if you died right now, would you go to heaven?" But, as Bell correctly observes, "Jesus doesn't tell people how to 'go to heaven.' It wasn't what

Jesus came to do" (p.30).

Love Wins speaks about the resurrect-ed body mentioned in 1 Corinthians 15. Then it says, "Prior to that, then, after death we are without a body. In heaven, but without a body.... Those currently 'in heaven' are not, obviously, here. And so they're with God, but without a body" (p. 56). These ideas come from the infiltration of Greek philo-sophy into the visible church in post-apostolic history, not from the OT/NT narrative. The NT views believers holistically, and sees them in *bodily* form. Paul repeatedly used the word "asleep" to describe the state of deceased believers. Asleep—awaiting resurrection day. It was a Greek notion that a person's spirit was trapped in the body, and the goal was for the spirit to be released at death. This alien conviction has saturated the visible church, and basically made our bodily resurrection superfluous. What do these scriptures mean? "And no one has ascended into heaven..." (John 3:13). "Brethren, I may confidently say to you regarding the patriarch David that he both died and was buried, and his tomb is with us to this day.... For it was not David who ascended into heaven..." (Acts 2:29, 34).

Think carefully about Matthew 25:31-46. All people—the just and the unjust—are gathered before Jesus, and he assigns the sheep and the goats to two separate destinies. Now, if all these people's body-less spirits had been in heaven or hell for long periods of time prior to this event, what sense would Jesus' words make to them? He would be informing them of what they already had known experientially for some time! What makes sense is dead bodies being resurrected and coming before King Jesus to be told of their destiny by the Lord. Please reflect on these questions: *How can a "person" be in Christ's presence without a body? How can a "spirit" be tormented in hell without a body*? (cf. "Then What?" Searching Together, 36:3-4, 2009; articles by David D. Flowers & W.F. Bell).

Universal Reconciliation or Eternal Torment?
Throughout *Love Wins* it is made to look like the only alternative to the "endless torment" position is it's universal reconciliation viewpoint

(pp. 1, 64, 67-68, 102). But that is not the case. I would like to suggest another alternative that, after years of study, possibly does the most justice to the images used in the NT. No position is airtight, and there are always a few scriptures that seem to challenge every view, including what follows, but please consider these points with me.

◊ When Sodom and Gomorrah were destroyed by fire, the inhabitants were not tormented forever. They were simply consumed by the fire from above. These two cities are an example, Peter and Jude noted, of the future judgment that will come upon the ungodly.

◊ The flood that the Lord sent upon the earth did not torture people forever, but after it accomplished its purpose, the waters receded. Peter notes that just as a water-judgment came upon the old creation, so now the current earth awaits a fire-judgment that will purge the earth of those who did not love Christ.

◊ Think of the images that are used in the NT regarding the final judgment. They are incongruous with the idea of "eternal torment." For example, in the parable of the wheat and tares, the reapers [angels] "first gather up the tares and bind them in bundles to burn them up" (Matt. 13:30). "Therefore," Jesus said, "just as the tares are gathered up and burned with fire, so shall it be at the end of the age" (Matt. 13:40). Hebrews 6 describes good ground that is blessed with vegetation, and then mentions ground that "yields thorns and thistles" and is "worthless and close to being cursed, and it ends up being burned" (v. 8). "If anyone does not abide in me," Jesus warned, "he is thrown away as a branch, and dries up; and they gather them, and cast them into the fire, and they are burned" (John 15:6). The burning described is not everlasting, but simply consumes that which is put in the furnace.

◊ There was a garbage dump southwest of Jerusalem called "Gehenna," the "valley of Hinnom." The fire in this place never went out, and the smoke never ceased, but the items thrown into this area would not burn forever, but be consumed slowly or quickly. Bell notes, "Wild animals fought over scraps of food along the edges of the heap. When they fought, their teeth would make a gnashing sound. Gehenna was the place with the gnashing of teeth, where the fire never went out" (p. 68).

◊ We need to pay attention to a word used in the famous John 3:16 that gets missed in the discussion of judgment. It is the word "*perish*"—"whoever believes in him should not perish." Check out in a concordance how this word is used. It means "to cease living," such as when the demon-possessed hogs went off the cliff and "*perished*." Unbelievers "perish"; believers have eternal life in Christ. The contexts where "perish" is used in the NT are incompatible with the idea of "eternal torment."

◊ The whole thing of a person's spirit leaving them when they die is based on the "immortal soul" doctrine. Everyone, it is alleged, has a "never-dying soul" that goes somewhere after death. This notion is rooted in Greek thinking, not in the biblical witness. The word "immortal" is used in the NT only of God, Christ and believers. To suggest that unbelievers are in any way "immortal" appears to be without Biblical warrant, and certainly has resulted in untold confusion. It seems to me that the totality of the biblical story would suggest that believers in Christ will be raised to immortality and eternal life with Christ, and those outside the Son will not be eternally tormented, but consumed by fire.

Love Wins presents it's view as a counter to the eternal torment position. But the viable option I have outlined was not considered. The view rejected by *Love Wins* teaches that "when you die…the torture and anguish and eternal torment will have just begun" (p. 64). This means, as someone in Rob's church suggested, that Mahatma Ghandi is in "hell" right now (p. 1). I don't think so. It seems most likely that no one is in heaven or hell right now. If people are currently in such places, then the scene given in Matthew 25:31-47 makes Jesus look pretty ignorant. He would just be announcing final destinies to people who already had been experiencing them for some time!

I have only scratched the surface concerning death and resurrection. A full and superb treatment can be found in Edward Fudge's *The Fire That Consumes: A Biblical and Historical Study of the Doctrine of Final Punishment* (3rd Ed., Wipf & Stock, 2011).

2 Thessalonians 1:4-10

You would think that if an author was going to posit the ultimate salvation of everyone, that a careful survey of all or many of the relevant "contrary" contexts that would be given. But *Love Wins* uses selected scriptures in such a way as to build a case, and does not interact with other Biblical perspectives that seem to call it into question. Paul's thought in 2 Thessalonians 1:4-10 would be an example of a context in conflict with the major points in *Love Wins*. Here's what Paul said to persecuted saints:

> Therefore, we ourselves speak proudly of you among the churches of God for your perseverance and faith in the midst of all your persecutions and afflictions which you endure. This is a plain indication of God's righteous judgment so that you will be consider-

ed worthy of the kingdom of God, for which indeed you are suffering. For after all it is only just for God to repay with affliction those who afflict you, and to give relief to you who are afflicted and to us as well, when the Lord Jesus will be revealed from heaven with his mighty angels in flaming fire, dealing out retribution to those who do not know God and to those who do not obey the gospel of our Lord Jesus. These will pay the penalty of eternal destruction, away from the presence [face] of the lord and from the glory of his power, when he comes to be glorified in his saints on that day, and to be marveled at among all who have believed—for our testimony to you was believed. (2 Thessalonians 1:4-10, *NASB*)

The saints in Thessalonica were experiencing deep affliction from unbelievers. Paul comforts them by looking forward to a time when the Lord would repay with intense judgment those who hurt the brothers and sisters. This would occur, Paul asserted, when the Lord Jesus would return in glory. Two major events would cluster around Jesus' appearance: (1) those who do not know God or the gospel will be punished with destruction away from the Lord's face; (2) those who know Jesus will be glorified and marvel in their Savior.

This passage clearly reveals a number of perspectives that highlight the difficulties with the position presented in *Love Wins*. (1) This coming of Jesus in glory terminates what we call "history." "This age" is over and the "age to come" is being inaugurated. (2) When history ends, there is a group of people who have not known God or obeyed the gospel. (3) These people are banished forever from the "face of the lord." (4) *Love Wins* believes that people will still have many chances to be reconciled after they die (pp. 79, 91, 105, 106). But in light of this passage, to posit that such people will have many opportunities to "find God" after Jesus' return is ruled out. (5) There is nothing in this context to suggest, as Bell does (p. 85), that the purpose of this future judgment is to "correct" persons and thereby "wrongdoers will become right doers" in the age to come (p. 91). (6) Paul did not comfort the afflicted saints by saying that in the future their tormentors would be reconciled to God. Rather, he comforted them by saying they would be "paid back" for touching God's anointed ones—the "millstone" principle. (7) While Christ's people are "glorified" (immortality), those outside the gospel are "destroyed" (burned up).

What Do "Perish" and "Destroy" Mean?

I invite you to use a Bible concordance and look up how the words "perish" and "destroy" are used in the NT. Right in the midst of the famous John 3:16 it states that the ones who believe should not perish but have everlasting life. Can "perish" mean "be tormented for ever and ever"? The answer seems to be, "Very unlikely." *Cruden's Complete Concordance* gave these thoughts on "destroy": "of demolishing buildings or cities; of putting an end to anything; of killing a person or persons; of nullifying."[2] These two key words used with reference to the fate of those outside of Christ do not mesh well with the meaning "to be tormented forever."

[2] Holt, Rinehart, Winston, 1965, pp. 144-145, 491; cf. W.E. Vine, *An Expository Dictionary of New Testament Words*, Revell, 1966, Vol. 1, p. 302; Vol. 3, pp. 176-177.

Is It Only About Love?

The first sentence of *Love Wins* states, "First, I believe that Jesus' story is first and foremost about the love of God for every single one of us" (p. vii). If what he says is true, is it not potentially very odd that the Jesus story was told repeatedly to numerous people groups in the Book of Acts, *and the word "love" is not used one time*? I do not say this to discount the presence of God's love in the Gospel, but just to point out that perhaps today's conception of the Gospel has swung to an isolated emphasis that was unknown in the first decade of expansion in the 1st century.

What About Wrath?

Another dimension that is undeveloped in *Love Wins* is the NT revelation concerning God's wrath. Not a pleasant subject for sure, but we are not at liberty to turn a deaf ear to what was mentioned a number of times by the NT writers. At the end of the chapter in John that contains "God so loved the world..." is this fact: "the one who disobeys the Son shall not see life, but the wrath of God abides on that person" (John 3:36).

In Romans, Paul asserted that "the wrath of God is revealed from heaven against all ungodliness…, because of your stubbornness and unrepentant heart, you are storing up wrath for yourself in the day of wrath and revelation of the righteous judgment of God… but to those who are selfishly ambitious… wrath and indignation…on the day when, according to my gospel, God will judge all secrets through Christ Jesus" (Rom. 1:18; 2:5, 8, 16). Paul reminded the Ephesian believers that before they knew Christ they "were by nature children of wrath, even as the rest" (Eph. 2:3). "How you turned to God from idols to serve a living and true God," Paul said to the Thessalonian believers, "and to wait for His Son from heaven, whom He raised from the dead, that is Jesus, who delivers us from the wrath to come" (1 Thes. 1:9-10). He went on to tell them, "For God has not destined us for wrath, but for obtaining salvation through our Lord Jesus Christ" (1 Thes. 5:9).

Don't Paul's words, along with others that could be mentioned, indicate rather forcefully that God's wrath rests upon fallen, unbelieving humans? Isn't there a day of judgment in the future in which his wrath will be expressed toward unbelieving persons? Why isn't this perspective touched upon in *Love Wins*? Given what is stated in many scriptures, is it proper to allow an understanding of God's love to swallow up any consideration of his anger against those who deny his Son?

I'm assuming *Love Wins* does not intend to do this, but it seems to me that its views have the end result of minimizing the value of Christ. It is as if not believing in Christ in one's lifetime is not really that big of a deal. It is as if there are no consequences for not embracing the Son in this age—no wrath, no judgment to come. But Paul exclaimed, "now is the day of salvation." There are no second chances. Psalm 2 said, "Kiss the Son, lest he be angry, and you perish in the way." How would 1 Corinthians 16:22 find meaning and reality in *Love Wins*? "If anyone does not love the Lord, let him be accursed. Maranatha."

Bad Story vs. Good Story

Love Wins feels that a tale in which countless people find endless torment "isn't a very good story" (p. 110). However, as I have pointed out, this view is not the only alternative to his idea of everyone being saved. "Everybody enjoying God's good world together," *Love Wins* goes on to say, "with no disgrace or shame, justice being served, and all wrongs being made right is a better story" (p. 111). It seems that *Love Wins* is more focused on a "better world" than on the glory of the King of Kings. How does Paul's future scenario unveiled in 1 Thess-alonians 1:4-10 fit into *Love Wins* "better story"? It seems instead to flatly contradict Paul's depiction of the future.

The way *Love Wins* interprets things, "What Jesus does is declare that he, and he alone, is saving everybody" (p.155). There are, however, a number of Scriptural contexts that will not validate such a vision. Certain persons being separated forever from "the face of God" (2 Thes. 1:9) does not sound like everybody "makes it."

The main thesis of *Love Wins* does not seem substantiated by all of the information in the Biblical story. One can hold to a vision of universal reconciliation—some in the past certainly have—but in order to do this, it would seem that significant portions of Christ's revelation must be ignored or re-shaped.

This raises an important question about how we use the Bible. There are verses that speak of "all things being reconciled in Christ," and there are many verses that talk about a judgment day for the wicked. *Love Wins* seems to absorb the judgment verses into the reconciliation verses, and end up with a theology where everyone ends up in bliss. Wouldn't it be a fairer use of scripture to take the multiple witness of so many verses about judgment seriously, and view them against the promise of a new heaven and new earth— where there will be no more sin, no more curse, no more tears, and no more wicked ones because they will be destroyed from the face of the Lord forever?

Of course, we could wish that the Lord's purposes in Christ left no one out. But if the NT is taken earnestly, such a wish does not appear to conform to reality. One important reason why many would be drawn to the main thesis of this book is the strong pull of our heartstrings regarding loved ones who now have no interest, or did not appear in the past to have had any interest in Jesus Christ. We need to keep in mind two facts. First, we do not know anyone's heart. It is not for us to police who is in Christ and who isn't. As long as humans have breath, there is hope. Secondly, we can know with certainty that "the Judge of all the earth will do right" (Gen. 18:25). The Lord knows those who are his.

Martin Luther rightly noted that there would be three huge surprises in the age to come —the people he thought would be there that aren't; the people he thought would never be there who are; and the biggest surprise of all: that he would be there!

FOR FURTHER REFLECTION

Fernando Ajith, *A Universal Homecoming?* Madras, India: Evangelical Literature Service, 1982.

Christian History, "The History of Hell: A Brief Survey & Resource Guide," Jennifer Trafton, project editor, 2011, 30 pp.

William Crockett, *Four Views of Hell*, Zondervan, 1997, 192 pp.

Oscar Cullmann, *Immortality of the Soul or Resurrection of the Dead? The Witness of the New Testament*, London: The Epworth Press, 1960, 60 pp.

Edward Fudge, *The Fire That Consumes: A Biblical and Historical Study of the Doctrine of Final Punishment*, Third Edition, Wipf & Stock, 2011.

Richard Gaffin, Jr., *The Centrality of the Resurrection — A Study in Paul's Soteriology*, Baker Biblical Monograph, Grand Rapids, Michigan (1978).

Jon Meacham, "Is Hell Dead?" *Time*, April 25, 2011, pp. 38-43.

J. Peter Nixon, "Has Hell Frozen Over?" *U.S. Catholic*,
November, 2011.

Dennis L. Okholm, *Four Views On Salvation in a Pluralistic
World*, Zondervan, 1996, 288 pp.

Marius Reiser, *Jesus & Judgment: The Eschatological Proclama-
tion in Its Jewish Context*, Fortress Press, 1997, 398 pp.

Searching Together, "What Next?" 36:3-4, 2009, 32 pp.;
articles by David D. Flowers and W.F. Bell.

Maurice Smith, *All Dogs Go To Heaven Don't They? Biblical
Reflections on Christian Universalism & Ultimate Reconciliation*,
2010, 262 pp.

Charles J. Wilhelm, *Biblical Dyslexia: Overcoming the Barriers
to Understanding Scripture*, Xulon Press, 2004, 195 pp.

ACKNOWLEDGEMENTS

I would like to thank the following people for their invaluable help in this project: *Kathy Huff, Bonnie Jaeckle, Michael Morrell, Brad Peterson, Rafael Polendo, Timothy L. Price, Marv and Jodi Root,* and *Cindy Skillman.*

Also, a hardcopy of this manuscript was sent by Certified Mail to Rob Bell. He was given the opportunity to read this material, and an invitation was extended to him to respond, if he wished.

CPSIA information can be obtained at www.ICGtesting.com
Printed in the USA
LVOW010957130112

263730LV00002B/1/P